Sit Here In The Smoke

Sit Here In The Smoke

Poems by Drue Stinnett

I give you my heart and tell you
the sun has blessed it,
the mountains named it,
and the birds sing
it home every evening.

Indigo

There was once a horizon
and then there was me.
A dancing child in the great big blue
with clouds for eyes and rain drops.

There was once a sky and I was
everything it had ever tasted.
I was the wind. I was the tide.
I was the moon.

There was once an ocean, deeper
and more wild than anything I had
ever known. Swallowing whole
anything brave enough to touch it.

Who really knows which
reflected the other?

What parts of this were
also parts of me?

Which parts of this
was I allowed to keep?

I grew mountains from my teeth.
Sequoias from my knees.
Streams and rivers from my cheeks.
I created everything.

So, if I should die sweep up these
sky-colored pieces
and pack them away with your
memory of me.

If I should change into someone
you cannot recognize,
paint the sky with the
indigo hue of this girl

you used to know. Don't call
me beautiful but call me blue.
Call me glass bottles.
Call me ocean water.

Call me summer six a.m.
when everything
was covered in me.

My depression

is a haunted artist and the nights
in which I do not dream about her
are few.

The sick makes my art

This morning, your hand swept
between my shoulder blades and
with a kiss on the cheek you ask if I
remembered to take my medicine.

This is a question in three parts.
First, the love. The you taking care
of me and the comfort I find in that.
Second, the sting.

The memory that I rely on small
white pills to control my mind so I
don't do things like run into traffic
or forget to sleep for three days.

The burn when I think about life
before the medicine. The long
nights. The darkness in my room
because I would never let you turn

on the lights. The poems,
all of the poems I could never read
out loud because they scared
everyone I knew.

Every day is a fight because some days I hold the pills in my palm and think about not getting better because the sick makes my art.

Because the sick is part of me. Because bipolar disorder is sometimes the most interesting thing about me

and what is left when that is gone I asked you once. You did not answer. You did plant me beautiful things like orange trees

and good lattes and every kiss we have ever shared and the feeling you get on warm afternoons

when the breeze comes at the perfect time.You painted memories. Mountains. Late-night drives. Walking to the edges of our world

and back again.
A good therapist. An exit sign
pointing me away from suicide.
You gave me every reason

I needed to swallow my pride
with that pill. You gave me beautiful
things. You told me there are no
interesting stories in which the

protagonist leaves in the middle of
the plot. No paintings remembered
when the artist gives up.
You told me I am enough.

This morning, when you ask if
I remembered, I nod into dishwater
and say yes.
Thank you for everything

you have ever done for me,
for drawing me the sun
in the middle of the night,
for helping me find my reasons

for staying alive

and making sure your name

was not the only thing on the list.

On mindfulness

I no longer apologize on behalf of
the trauma. My world is not a
museum of what is broken.

My writing is done
being a cemetery of nightmares.
It is a good day to be alive.

I have not erased what happened,
but I do not call it
"what was done to me".

It does not have ownership
over this body anymore.
The pain is not in a box,

but I do not let it pull me
into its dark abyss. I see it, feel it,
but do not fight it.

I cannot lose if I do not play.
The sun kisses me every morning,
and I do not mean a boy,

but the actual sun.
The dark days are not
the thick of my plot.

There are no dark days
when stars line every path.

Shoelace

When I think about dying,
I think about my shoelace.
When it breaks, no one
ever really expects it
no matter how old the shoes are.

When I think about the snap
and the cursing,
I think about August heat
and being fourteen
in a church, tasting the bitterness
of the first life lost in my memory.

When I think about dying,
I think about tequila and the burn
down my throat when I was sixteen.
Cigarette smoke in my lungs
and the scarred wrists of the boy
who bought them for me.

When I think about the burn,
I think about the tattered couch
where everything changed, about
the way I held my breath and tasted
the world for the first time.

When I think about dying,
I think about the box of
photographs we found
in my grandpa's closet after his
funeral. Black, white, and faded
until the faces were nearly a
mystery.

When I think about the candids,
I think about scrubbing the smell of
beer out of my favorite shirt until
I was sure my mother wouldn't
notice when I walked into the
house.

When I think about dying,
I think about every drive that was
too fast around curves and the
adrenaline from every first kiss.

When I think about dying,
I think about my shoelace
and hope that when it one day
breaks, it won't matter if I was
expecting it.

Bodies

there is no warmth
in the limp casket
wrapped in white linen
at the edge of my bed.

her body dressed
in familiar sadness.
open eyes glazed
against the ceiling fan,

searching for a version
of herself that
was once alive.
a frame of bones and skin,

once a heated
home on a
white winter morning.

Sacrilegious

I am an empty church.
Something once beautiful,
now desolate and depressed
and everything sad in the world.

My church had stained glass
windows of Jesus.
Those windows are now shattered
on the outside grass.

The glass cuts my feet when I flee
from the home that raised me
on praise songs and prayer.
A burning reminder that

I did not turn out the way
I was intended to.
I did not praise
the moon and call it Christ.

I did not ask for sins
to be erased, but instead
celebrated them for the sheer
humanity in nakedness

and tongues.
My chapel is your bedroom.
Linen soft on my shoulders, the only
place I have ever called safe

and meant it so.
I tithe my time and mouth.
My mind plays the greatest
offering in your pulpit.

I give you my heart and tell you
the sun has blessed it,
the mountains named it,
and the birds sing
it home every evening.

Flash flood

Be sure to put your faith in
someone faithful.
Someone willing to stay while
waves wipe out every beautiful
thing you have ever known.
Be sure that they can close
the shutters on their own heart
before storms roll in.
That they can stand with you.
That they will stand with you in the
middle of the ocean.
I will stand on the shore
begging you not to leave me
behind.

Vacancy sign

My tongue is a shingle tarred to the
roof of my mouth.
My mouth is the tallest building in
this skyline of things

you love to see but hate the
commitment of living in.
My throat cracks like the dried
concrete lining your walk back to

the hotel room you are renting here.
There are no flowers. Just dust.
Dust in the curtains long drawn
over sunlit windows.

Dust in the carpet I haven't
cleaned since you moved here.
Dust in the way you say "I love you"
as we roll tongues into goodnight.

I would checkout early, too
even though this bed is so
comfortable with you in it.
Knees knocking in sheets

like bumper cars driven
by young, drunk girls.
We hit and we laugh.

Near Mother's Day

Aren't we all the poetry of our
mother's breasts?
Are we not stanzas of life?
Of survival? Of heart?
Of course, we are bred in iron.

Fierce and strong like the hips
that carried us and the arms that
soothed our hungry cries;
our first moments of loneliness.

Mama, I am lonely.
Have you been this lonely?
Where are those hands
freckled and tanned
from watermelon summertime?

The hands that could fix anything.
Every scrape of my knee.
Every heart broken by a boy.
Every ripped seam on skirts or

broken toys.
Every blow to my self-esteem.
Mama, you are poetry.
You are glowing.

You are lonely and raw
with the power of a lion
and the love of spring
and all of her blooming beauty.

Aren't we all too forgetful that
Mama is human.
Mama is lonely.
That Mama tries her damn hardest
for us to be so blinded by her
superhero costume

We don't remember
that her hands
were just like our hands
before our hands
were ever formed.

Nineteen

You are cold now. A snow storm
in June with no coat to slip into.
Your mind races, burning through
trauma. The fire is keeping you alive

and it is killing you. You stand on
the top-tier of a parking deck,
making the whole world feel so
small, wondering when will you

be able to sleep in a man's arms
without feeling like you have to
clench a knife to your chest so
that you may slice your own wrists
before he has the chance to.

Nocturne

This spilled-ink sky is decorated
with a mess of slaughtered stars,
and their dust reminds me of you
and of the way you slaughtered me.

of the way I felt the astrological
composition of my body collapse
when I realized you did not love me.

every universe, every alternate
reality fell into each other the way I
fall into others when
I drink Bacardi. Clumsy.

the way you fall into bed when you
are tired. the way the world
crumbled in your palm.
on your tongue.

you kept living and I
am still writing you poetry.
and you will never read this.
you don't even like poems.

you said they are easy
like you said I was easy
as though you did not pry me open
beneath a spilled ink sky.

as though I did not stare at
slaughtered stars
while my body's astrological
composition fell apart

I spent three years eulogizing my
eighteen-year-old heart,
grieving the loss of
innocence and childhood.

Today, I left pink rose petals where
you held me to the ground.
their blushing stems form
a blanket on the side

of the curvy mountain road where
 you killed me.
"I'm sorry,"
I speak to my ghost on the leaves.
"One day, you will continue living."

Summer carpet, 2017

It is warm. The sun is hovering
right above the mountain tops.

My mother is washing dinner dishes
and I want to shake her awake

and tell her that all I can
think about is killing myself.

But I sit, glued to my bedroom
carpet and continue to get over it

like I have gotten over it for the last
eight years. Praying to a god

I'm not sure exists.
Praying I remain so lucky.

Thirteen days

Today, I wrote four things
on a to do list.
By six p.m., they are each
checked and I am silent.

A deep breath for my
often-deprived lungs.
I feel my heartbeat
but it does not worry me.

I made dinner plans and
remembered to go to them.

I made a house of cards
for my depression
and I did not leave
the key under the rug.

I look at my calendar.
I touch the days
like they are water.
I count every drop to tally

the number of days it has been
since I was going to kill myself.

There is a fist crawling up my
throat. I hold my breath
until it disappears. I check the
syllabi for my classes.

I am no longer falling behind
but I am falling in love
with the ability to move my arms
and wake up to my alarms

I have found this sacred
middle ground after years of
thinking you must be one
or the other.

I speak calmly.
My thoughts come to me calmly.

Today was a good day.

Lullaby

there are no truths
in the deceptive teeth
of melancholic bedtime greetings.
when darkness slips a satin noose
around your neck and tells you
it is a pillowcase.

Water balloon

Am I in love with you or the feeling
of being in love with you?
Because if I am in love
with you that means
there is something left in me.

Lately, I've felt empty.
Like a water balloon
pricked open and dripping into
autumn grass, left behind
from the summer heat.

Maybe, with some work,
I could be full again-
but who really has the time?
It's so much easier to lay here
and drip – drip – drip away from
anything that makes me feel
anything.

and you're here, like the
water hose coiled up and ready to
pass on all the things
I need to feel full again.

but here's the problem:

I've still got this pin prick and
nothing can stay for too long.

but there is a linger. a whisper
in my ear every time I feel like
leaving and all I can smell
is your cologne

and for a moment I feel
like my heart as eaten
three thanksgiving dinners.
and I might bust open from all of
 the *things* that I *feel.*

and it tells me
there is something
worth staying for.

Ideation

I text my boyfriend. I tell him
I've been laying in the floor
for three hours. I tell him I'm
shivering

because that sounds so much
nicer than saying "I'm convulsing."

I tell him I'm cold but I'm wondering
if I'm even alive because everything,
even the rug under my elbows feels
like a distant memory.

my mouth never moves but it feels
like I'm shrieking out for someone
to help me.
he asks if he can do anything and I
tell him I don't know

but I actually do know
and I actually do know that the only
thing
that might help me is breaking glass
instead of thinking.

watching chards of mason jars
fill the sidewalk like my depression
fills my mouth and cuts.

the way mania wraps her fingers
around my brain until it collapses.
and I am crushed by my emotions.

the way suicide is so foreign until
I'm in my bed
playing with pills and mourning
what could have been.
the way that there is a crash

and I am cold on the floor thinking
 about a single word.

The room

I feel the walls of our love closing in.
Everything is getting tighter and we
are being pushed against each
other and the air is hot and wet
as we breathe
through each other's lungs.

it hurts. my chest is heavy and my
ribs are stretching to accommodate
this, even when there is no room
for my body to open.

i press into your arms – strong and
crossed over your chest in a
defiant, quiet stare.

maple syrup brunch sticks to my
fingers and i pray into your ear,
kiss me, kiss me, kiss me
with your crushed velvet lips,

purple from the way this room
is sinking in.

Close quarters

if absence
makes the heart grow fonder

how do these
broom-closet heartaches

feel in the
back of your mind?

are you still
in love with only being mine

when you cannot
see the dusk-dusted sky?

The haunting

Here, I am the room.
I am the furniture.
I am the flame
burning everything down.

I made mounds on my carpet
using every piece of
clothing I own. I am a burglar
in my own home.
Only taking reality and leaving
things unclear.

There are bloodstains
from my favorite lipstick.
I hang caution tape around the
manic craft project.
My bones lay in a circle, like a
mausoleum in my living room.

I am the ghost.
I am the funeral.
I am the murder scene.

My hands are small daggers that
cut through everything.
My skin. My bones. My sheets.
Nothing is safe from the fire
because I am the gasoline.

I stare into mirrors and see no
reflection. There is nothing here
but the clothes on the carpet
and a heartbeat connected to
something empty.

God forgive the way I'm letting
myself burn.
God forgive the way I lit the
kindling.
God forgive the way I will never
forgive myself.

I'll sit here in the smoke alone.

No witnesses.
No victims.
No crime.

When I talk about being depressed

I am told to look at beauty
around me.
Stay awake for the sunrise,
for the spring blooms on my
favorite flower bush,

For freshly ground coffee, for
weddings
and sand and fresh air. To tell them
I love them again.
To hear them sing.

Stay here for beautiful things, I hear.
Stay for one more chance
at finding joy. I say it's bad.
They say it's beauty. I say it's rain,
they say

the sun will come again.
I say my heart beats like
an old, broken car engine.
They say at least it's beating still.

I want to scream, but I see
no one sees me. No one hears.
No one can listen to the grief
because
they only want to solve it.

They can't listen without fixing.
but my mourning needs to sing to
an audience,
ever how small. Ever how sorry.
Ever how pained.

I feel that too, I tell them.
I feel that hurt so deep inside of
myself that I can no longer tell
where I end and it begins.

It's been there since I was a kid,
I say. It's been that way forever.
I'm sick. I'm sick. I'm sick.
My brain - my own fucking
head – is sick

and I need you to tell me nothing.
You can't catch this cold.
You can't spread my germs
to your family. You are safe.

God, I can't remember what that
feels like.
Don't you see how dark even the
sunniest mornings are when you are
stuck
mourning the person you used to
be?

You lost without knowing
she was going. You lost
without saying goodbye
or please stay.

A Waltz

The monster under the bed does
not go away as you get older,
he just becomes more real, and
more inside your head
all at once.

I have to sleep with my lights on
to keep the dark away,
so the space in my head is clear of
my monster.

He tells me so many things in a
voice like wine. It's sweet.
It stains. It's so easy to say
"one more glass."
He tells me that death
is sweeter than here.
Sweeter than suffering.

He tells me that I am suffering.
There are no reasons.
I just am. I just suffer.

And cry.

He tells me this is the next best
thing to getting black-out drunk
and laying on my carpet but even
he knows I'm too broke for that.

So I weep more days than not.
I cry to jazz and let the saxophones
coat me in syrup until I am asleep
in my puddle. Asleep in my pain.

Not wondering if these
tears are real
or just part of the game
I play with the monster
under my bed.

The Leaving

i wish you carolina.
open doors to pine trees and navy
beaches. never too far from the
hope of home

hope that strangers smile
back the way you always do here.

i wish you no strangers,
but family you didn't know
you knew until you met them.

i wish you long memories
and a pen with which to write them.

i wish you no contentment
but a life of constant going
and finding new doors.

i wish you endless mountains and
everything you need to climb them.

i wish you carolina in every direction
and everywhere you need a home.

On the weather

Today, I read a study that found
tropical storms named after women
kill more people than storms
named after men.

I read that male names heed
strength and fear and people
always take them more seriously
and all of this leads me to wonder

if my name is why no one, not even
me, takes the brewing hurricane
inside of my stomach seriously.

I can feel my bones quiver
and I can feel my joints get stiff –
just like when the weather gets
rough but instead of cold rain

there are heat waves
in my fan-cooled bedroom. Heat
waves until my floor turns into
a pool of sweat.

Heat waves because my brain
is so caught up in the worry and the
racing that it cannot regulate my
body. It can't tell the difference

between this carpet and hell and
neither can I sometimes.
I just want to be cold one more
time. Feel rain one more time.

See flowers, unwilted,
unhurt from the blaze.

Unsolicited advice on romance

they say love is blind, but have they
ever been in love?
love is seeing everything
for the first time.
that which you thought
you knew is nothing.
that which you now know
is a golden world unfolded.
this love and every one
after it will be a new vision
that will change
entire universes
every constellation
every interaction
every heartbeat
and why it matters.

Alex

An SJW walks into a bar
and a man is sitting
with a neat whiskey in his hand
and he curls his lip to spit
on the seat beside him.

SJW clasps her hands
and waits -not for a slur
but just for her drink

and Spitting Man coughs it all on
the counter -

"These are my politics.
This is my country.
This is my language.
This is my constitutional
right to tell you-"

He turns to SJW, finger-wagging
in a seated, drunken stumble.

"You look like a feminist bitch.
Like a snowflake bitch.
Like a safe zone, queer-friend,
Black Lives Matter
bitch."

A deep breath quipped
and knocking back
the last of his liquor -

"Hillary-voting,
organic chicken,
move to Portland,
Occupy bitch."

SJW flashes a smile,
nods and raises her glass.

"Thank you.
Thank you very much."

On healing

Tell me about a time someone
hurt you. We're talking knife
in the gut and twist.
Hammer to your heart and drag.

You would never recover
because everything
that had ever mattered
was shattered.

Tell me about how your art
saved you. Tell me about the
photo lens, felt-tipped pens,
bleeding in to cure
your bleeding heart.

Tell me about heartache.
The hollowness in your chest
when you realize your last kiss
was the real last kiss.

Tell me about hope.
About today.
About the future you dreamt of
but never thought you would get.

Tell me about happiness.
Tell me how, after all of this,
you still seem so
okay?

***Thirteen things every woman
needs in her handbag***

lip stick.

breath mints.

pepper spray.

hand lotion.

a key ring that will fit over your hand
like a weapon. tissues.

Target coupons.

a stun gun that looks

like a smartphone.

your house key.

the regret you bear

for being a woman.

the regret you bear

for regretting being

a woman.

a book to read on the bus.

a bookmark that

is also a blade.

you will not feel safe without it.

Hallucinations

On my walk home today
the pavement turned
into black snakes.

I walked across them anyway,
only scared I might hurt
them under my shoes.

I made it all the way across
campus. I never even looked for
cars before

I crossed streets or parking lots. It's
not that I want to die. I just don't
know that I want to be alive, either.

Suicide will always have a seat at
the table. This doesn't mean
I have to fill its plate.

Risk

I've been thinking lately
about taking chances,
taking risks.

I've been thinking about
all of the things that have long
Seemed out of reach.

I want to gountil I'm far
from here. So far that I don't
Exist to anyone

or anything but the stars
in the sky and the white lines
on the curving roads

that guide me on a trip
I'm not even sure
I'm taking.

Goodnight kiss

The words "I love you"
are suddenly closure.

A door lock clicking,
a noose tightening,

A goodbye, a finale,
coffee spilling down the drain.

It sounds like
"you're the only one I ever loved."

Sounds like
"I'm sorry I'm doing this to you."

Sounds like "Move on quickly."

Sounds like "Please don't be mad."

1-800-273-8255

National Suicide Prevention Line

Wildfire

Today, I felt every part of my body
unravel like old yarn.
Untied. Nothing but fragments
of a broken composition.

I want to remember the sunshine.
I want to remember warmth.
I want to remember water.
Sweetness. Softness.

Not crashing. Not hurting.
Not darkness. Not cold.
Not brokenness.
I crave peace.

Like it's cold water and I am
trapped in a desert. Like it is a fire
and I am laying in a midnight forest.

My body is not mine today.
I don't know my mind is either.
Everything I touch is up in flames.
Nothing can be saved from the
blaze.

An unpredicted ending

I give everything back now,
former love of my life.
Every kiss. Every drive.
Every gentle caress above the
elbow in large crowds.

Every moment I swore
I would love you until the end,
not realizing that this
would be the bitter early ending

of a love once so dear to me.
This is a love now so dead to me.
Aching bones and aching hearts

and the baseball bat
on my glass heart
that pounds at me, telling me
to take everything back from you.

And the predicted one

I think I'm losing you, but how
much of that is me losing myself in
hallucinated memories
of what my life could be.

What good am I if all I have
to offer are twisted projections of
someone else's sheets and
constructions of paper dreams
alongside love letters from years in
your garden?

Darling, I am the poison that may
not kill you but without doubt will
kill all hope my life has left
and kill all time leading
to the end of us and all we could
have been.

I am in love, but since when was
that not enough to hold on or put
 up a fight or hold up my glass to
toast a romance as sweet as this.

Home

Amber musk and faded t-shirts
against my morning skin
and we are alive
and there is a sun

and for the first time
in a long time
all is well.

On the leaving

everything is changing and i didn't
know where you fit

your hand here in the place
it has always belonged.

your hand here palm-to-palm.
a shift in the tectonics of our world

and suddenly i couldn't tell the
greatness

from the tragedy
the happiness from the lonely.

everything is changing and i
couldn't see

where exactly you
needed me to be.

About the author

Drue Stinnett is a native to western
North Carolina with a passion for
crafting stories worthy of attention
in our media-saturated world.

A scholar of communication and
sociology, she found her love of
poetry when she was a first-year
college student.

Her writings focus on mental health,
relationships, and self-reflection.

For more of her work, be sure to
grab a copy of her first self-
published collection, *Propinquity.*

www.ingramcontent.com/pod-product-compliance
Lightning Source LLC
Chambersburg PA
CBHW030853090426
42737CB00009B/1216